RICH HALL'S
VANISHING AMERICA

RICH
HALL'S

VANISHING AMERICA

Macmillan Publishing Company • *New York*

To Marianne,
"You Got It, Mister."

Macmillan Publishing Company
866 Third Avenue, New York, N.Y. 10022
Collier Macmillan Canada, Inc.

Library of Congress Cataloging in Publication Data
Hall, Rich, 1954–
Rich Hall's vanishing America.
I. Title. II. Title: Vanishing America.
PN6162.H26 1986   814'.54   86-12842

ISBN 0-02-547480-4

10 9 8 7 6 5 4 3 2 1
PRINTED IN THE UNITED STATES OF AMERICA

Graphics by Bob Pook
Designed by Antler & Baldwin, Inc.

CONTENTS

How to Leave 7

The Shopping Center 8

The Bear 15

A Short-Hop History 17

Texaco Tannhäuser 19

Soap for One 25

Spap-Oop 29

The Poseidon Party 32

Shoe in the Road 39

The Good Guy 45

A Fine Sight to See 49

Drop in Any Mailbox 53

Charley 57

The P & C Man 60

5¢ to a Dollar 66

Some Women I've Known 72

Fred Suss's Ship in a Can 74

The Hardest Working Voice in Show Business 77

Thwop, Thwop 82

Ridiculous 86

"Zing" 90

Home 93

Glenn 96

The Ugliest Town in America 103

Lucy 109

Special Thanks to 112

HOW TO LEAVE

It isn't that hard to walk out.

"I'm stepping out for a pack of cigarettes," I say, and you know I'm leaving because I don't smoke.

Nope. It's not that hard.

Especially because I'm a young urban failure.

Because all my friends have married, moved on, keep promising to have me over for dinner sometime.

Because I've been staring at the same apartment walls for eleven years. The plumbing stain. The *Desiderata* poster.

It's not that hard.

I've just got around to reading *Rabbit Run*.

I say: "I'm stepping out for a pack of cigarettes." And I leave.

It's easy.

Especially since there's no one there to hear me.

THE SHOPPING CENTER

I grew up in the shadows of a shopping center.

It was my domain, my backyard, my battlefield, my commissary, my library. A place to prowl and daydream and squander whole chunks of my Wonder Years.

At least twice a week I conducted Free Sample Runs there. The tour began with a single butterscotch candy from the Brach's bin at Woolworth's. This was followed by an imported cracker and smudge of Danish Cheese Ball from Hickory Farms. Bresler's Ice Cream offered a smidgeon of any of their 31 Flavors. At the Nutrition Store there were soysticks, store-made peanut butter, and discs of Vitamin C at least as tasty as children's aspirin. I knew there was a fine line between sampling and filching, and I was careful not to cross it.

Appetite sated, I would stop by the Safeway and pick up a fistful of Greyhound Racing Forms (No Purchase Necessary), mentally noting my picks for all eight races, which were broadcast on TV each Saturday night at 6:00.

My last stop would be the hardware store where I would claim a wooden yardstick. Once outside, it made a terrific sword.

The shopping center was called Magnolia Acres. It was L-shaped with an awninged sidewalk, and fanned out to a herringboned parking lot.

• • •

It is still there today, but Hickory Farms is now The Croissant Corner, Bresler's (now called Jerome's) forces you to watch your ice cream being made in the storefront window, and Craddock's Hardware was sold to a pair of brothers named Stuart and Josh Lingerfelt who quickly installed twelve-thousand dollars worth of butcher-block display tables, renamed it The Provisory,

and featured only the Best tools and urban implements. The Lingerfelt Brothers previously sold log cabins in Vermont.

Magnolia Acres (three magnolias, seven acres) is in an older, revitalized section of town, which, depending on the Places-rated Almanac you consult, is the second, fourth, or sixteenth Most Livable City in America. The town has good schools and roads. It has a moderate climate. It has a few small problems, of course. The rising number of homeless people, for instance. And a rapidly lowering water table.

But all in all, it's a nice little Standard Metropolitan Statistical Area.

•   •   •

The shopping center is where I head right after I walk out. It's way across town. I haven't been there in years.

I go into Gaunces Newsstand. Amazingly, it has changed very little. There is a new magazine section titled, "Coffee Table Magazines." Other than that, it's pretty much as I remember. Old Gaunce still sits on a platform, gumming a Roi-Tan, timing browsers.

"Lookin' or buying?" he drones every fifteen seconds.

"Gimme a pack of cigarettes," I say.

"You don't smoke," he says, even though he hasn't seen me in seventeen years.

"I just walked out on myself. I'm pretty tense."

"What brand?"

"I don't know. What brand did Rabbit Angstrom smoke?" I am just testing him. It was never specified in the novel.

"Chesterfields."

"Fine."

He throws me a pack of Chesterfields, snaps a dollar from my fingers.

I grab some complimentary matches, glance at the cover. It shows an ad for return-address labels.

I walk back out to where my sad Corolla is parked.

I light up a Chesterfield and inhale.

The world starts spinning in a different direction.

•   •   •

There is a car parked in front of the Corolla, a pitted 1963 Buick Gunboat. The car belongs to a man named Ahmed. Ahmed is from Ankara, Turkey. All the possessions he owns in the New World sit in a bundle in the back seat of the Buick.

Ahmed has just conducted his own Free Sample Run.

Among the items he has collected is a coat hanger from the dry cleaners (which now offers something called French Hand Laundry and Expert Flatwork).

He is standing beside the Gunboat trying to figure out how to attach the hanger to where an antenna used to be.

You might say, since arriving in America, Ahmed has not been getting great reception.

I climb into my own car, reeling from the tobacco. While I'm maneuvering away from the curb, I bump the rear of Ahmed's Buick. The Buick pitches forward several feet. Ahmed turns and observes me curiously.

He remembers something someone had told him before departing for the United States: "In America, if someone hits you from behind, IT IS AUTOMATICALLY THEIR FAULT."

Ahmed falls to the ground and begins writhing in pain, screaming, "Whiplash!!"

Later he will also decide his foot has been run over.

•   •   •

When the police arrive, I try to explain that the man could not possibly have whiplash. He had not even been inside the car.

"So you're saying you hit him?" a cop asks.

"I hit the car."

"From behind?"

"Well, yes."

"Then, it's AUTOMATICALLY YOUR FAULT."

An ambulance pulls up and takes Ahmed to the hospital where he will enjoy three hot meals daily and remote-control television. This represents one less displaced person.

The police file their report and leave. Already, legislative wheels are in motion. By Monday afternoon the State Insurance Commission will have revoked my policy.

I start up my car. A thin geyser of green fluid spews from the radiator and begins its long seepage into the city's declining water table.

This is around 6:00 p.m.

The only tow-truck operator open on a Saturday afternoon is Mashburn's Shell, twenty-two miles away. The owner, Clinton Mashburn, makes the trip himself.

Clinton's route takes him past the brand-new Mountain Laurel Mineral Springs Waterworks, which at this moment is celebrating its Grand Opening. A handcarved sign shows a mountain stream gurgling through a cluster of alpine laurel. The mountain spring water has never seen a hint of mountain. It is tapped from a local aquifer three blocks away.

Clinton remembers when the place had been the home of a bear who specialized in wheel alignments.

.   •   .

The Shell station is from a bygone era. There is no glass booth and you don't have to sound like you're placing a bet ("five dollars on number three, please") when buying your gas. It is a full-service facility.

Clinton Mashburn sets my Toyota down among some other to-be-repaired autos. He goes inside to get a work form. I stroll idly among the cars.

One catches my eye. A 1955 Chevy, a two-door coupe. I smile. My first car had been a '55 Chevy.

Even rusted out, this car looks solid, low, and vicious.

I run a hand over the cannonesque quarter-panel, lean against the door, which is like a beefy shoulder. It rounds upward toward thick LOF Safety Glass. The slightest overhang of fender above headlight gives the car its distinctive "eyebrows." And the trademark taillights are like, well, ruby insets.

I remember the miles of pleasure behind the steering wheel of my own '55. Remember the feel of that wheel, small and thick, a tensed conduit to all the muscle lurking just beyond the firewall.

A strange sense of fondness washes over me. I feel *connected* to this car.

And when I peer inside I realize, this *is* my car.

I recognize it from small details. The tear in the headliner, the surfer foot, the bottle caps for radio dials.

I remember the day the car broke down.

It happened in a Greek neighborhood. There was a "bronk" and the car just stopped, like stunned big game. I climbed out to see 265 c.u.'s of engine lying underneath the car. Residents drifted from their porches, mutely eyeing me from a distance, whispering among themselves. No one could offer assistance, except, perhaps, the use of a phone, and when Clinton arrived with a winch, we solemnly watched the engine lowered onto his truck bed, like a child's casket. I didn't even accompany the car to the Shell station. I knew I would never be able to afford the repair. So I stood and watched the car disappear, a failure of heft and promise. Instantly I was a pariah. In suburban high school, without a car, you were nothing.

· · ·

"I thought that was you when I picked you up," Clinton says. "But I didn't say anything."

We are standing beside the Chevy.

"Greek neighborhood, wasn't it?"

"Yeah."

"You had a broken motor mount." He makes a "yea big" sign with his fingers indicating a piece of hardware about three inches wide.

"Cost three seventy-five."

"Three dollars and seventy-five cents?"

"Plus six-dollars labor. I quit trying to call you around nineteen seventy-seven."

· · ·

I pull away in the '55 feeling alive. There is no padding inside the car and the engine is deafening. The sound insulates. There is just me and the Chevy with that fine leftover Platformate coursing through its veins.

•   •   •

At exactly 7:00 p.m., the founder of the Mountain Laurel Waterworks issues a toast. Then his staff sets about bottling an initial five-thousand gallons of Mountain Spring Mineral Water. He opens a gate valve that draws directly from the town's aquifer.

The enormous demand causes an area of ground about ninety yards in circumference to cave inward. This is called a sinkhole.

The sinkhole is directly beneath a brand-new luxury condominium at 34 Irby Street. The condo is being constructed with 1 × 3s and Kleenex-strength insulation.

The condominium, thirty-four soon-to-be-occupied units, is sucked into the earth. Vanished.

I round the corner of Irby Street and see the last portion of the condo poking out of the ground.

I just keep on going.

THE BEAR

I drive all night.

The road begins to change, rising in elevation, becoming narrow and sinewy. In the dark I can make out the distant shapes of barns and satellite dishes, often side by side.

By sunup my eyes are dry and achy. I need some easy roadway. In America, you're never far from the interstate and I find it soon enough, easing down the entrance ramp.

Instantly I become truck sandwich-filling.

The one ahead has Yosemite Sam mudflaps. Sam's guns are drawn. "Back off," he snarls. But I can't. The semi behind will eat me.

Then the Chevy starts to act strangely. The front wheels buck and wobble like a manic shopping cart. The steering wheel fights my grip. The car seems to be in a fit.

I pull off at the next ramp, turn onto a two-lane.

Just like that, the conniptions stop.

I stop and climb out and walk around, examining the car with that kind of hopeful desperation that whatever's wrong is so slap-your-head silly that even a moron could fix it. I can't think of anything to do but kick a tire. When I look up there is a bear standing across from me.

I recognize him immediately as a Wheel Alignment Bear. Wheel Alignment Bears have yellow fur and a permanent, winsome grin. Not only do they fish and forage, they can calibrate, set toe and camber, and read a parts catalog. It's good to see they're still around.

The bear seems to be gesturing affably toward the underside of the Chevy. I drop to the pavement, peer underneath. I see then that the car has a Short-Hop Suspension.

A SHORT-HOP HISTORY

The Short-Hop Suspension was a package option available on certain cars in the mid-fifties. It was designed for short, pleasurable jaunts into the country, to the next town, or for stepping out for a pack of smokes.

It was made for back roads and small towns.

The official testing ground for the Short-Hop Suspension was a Dairy Queen parking lot in Michigan.

Like Platformate, which increased a car's mileage tenfold and spawned the "paper barrier run" craze among teens, the Short-Hop Suspension was a doomed marvel of engineering.

It disappeared around the time this slogan came out:

WATCH OUT FOR THE OTHER GUY

Before that, people tooled about happily, taking things in, enjoying themselves.

Suddenly, driving became defensive. Forget the sights and scenery, there was a crazy man over the next hill and he was drifting into your lane.

The Other Guy.

Who was this other guy? I wanted to meet him, but the government built huge, wide interstate highways to keep him at a distance.

To trap the other guy, they installed radar and Vascar and even claimed to patrol the roads with aircraft, though I never saw a plane swoop down and pull the Other Guy over.

They controlled his on-and-off access, and at the end of each exit ramp made everything the same. The places where the Other Guy ate and slept looked like Every Other Place.

The truth is, only on America's vanishing back roads can you still even glimpse the Other Guy. See the joy or boredom or wanderlust on his passing face.

So I've chosen to motor along these back roads, leisurely searching for the Other Guy, the Other Town, the Other Curio or Curiosity.

I'm going to see the USA in short-hops.

So watch out for me.

Because I'll be taking my own sweet time.

And if you hit me from behind . . . IT'S AUTOMATICALLY YOUR FAULT.

TEXACO TANNHÄUSER

FAUST, NORTH CAROLINA.

The Platformate ran out here.

· · ·

Faust, near Mt. Mitchell, is the windiest spot in Eastern America.

When they mention the weather in Faust, a lot of factoring has been taken in.

"Radio said it was sixteen."

"That's pretty cold for March."

"Of course, the windchill factor makes it seem like twenty below."

"Wow."

"In dog degrees that's one hundred and forty below."

The town is fiercely Germanic. There are three Lutheran churches. A bakery that serves something called pfeffernusse. There is an Oktoberfest (which, because of the cold, is held in late August).

There is no service station in Faust, but there is a *Gashaus*, where—if you're lucky—you might see a performance of Mallinkrodt's Texaco Tannhäuser Orchestra.

"Blow Horn for Service" reads a sign on the pump in front of the Gashaus, which is the first thing you come to when you are approaching Faust.

Inside, a face flashes at a window.

I honk. No one ventures out.

I honk again. Someone in a green uniform appears on the porch, head cocked curiously.

I wait. The wind whistles through the vent rubber of my window. Anvil-shaped clouds hustle across the sky, getting the hell out of North Carolina.

What gives? I blow the horn again, really lean on it. Finally the attendant in green trots over. I roll down the window.

"Play that again," says Frieda Mallinkrodt. Her face is brown and furrowed and burnished by years of cold, her hands calloused. Not the hands of a conductor.

"Play what?"

"That horn. Lemme hear it."

I blow the horn.

"An A," she says, her head cocked again. "That's a rare note for an automobile horn."

"This is a rare automobile."

The next thing I know I am sitting in with Mallinkrodt's Texaco Tannhäuser Orchestra.

As you might guess, this orchestra only knows one piece: *Tannhäuser.* Let Frieda Mallinkrodt explain:

"Tannhäuser was a knight. And a real crooner. He was summoned to heaven to perform for the gods, then thrown out for singing about mortals. Back on Earth he enters a singing contest, but gets thrown out of that for singing about gods. His problem, you see, was his poor choice of material. It's a sad, beautiful opera.

"We've carried Firestone tires for thirty-eight years," she

says. "Most folks don't equate tires with music, but Firestone used to put out Christmas albums, which we sold right there on a rack beside the Forty-Weight. The Voice of Firestone Symphony Orchestra performed on the radio every Monday. A very fine orchestra. Quite often there would be a Wagner selection. You can't understand the importance of Wagner to the people around here. It is a strong, bracing kind of music, and it helps people get through the winter. Well, something happened. The Orchestra quit playing and the tire company stopped making record albums, and we had to find a way to preserve Wagner for ourselves."

So they did.

·   ·   ·

It is around 4:30 in the afternoon, and the garage adjoining Frieda's house is filling fast. Classical music lovers pick their way around slick pools of oil and bob for a good view. The best seat is atop a portable hydraulic lift.

In a corner of the bay, eight or nine steering wheels, still attached to their columns, are suspended from a frame of 2 × 4's and sawhorses. The columns are connected to horns mounted about the shelves. This intricate setup is presided over by a man named Frank Anhalt. Roy Brietz and Bernard Tieter will accompany Frank on "frusenstogens," stringed instruments fashioned from cigar boxes and ice scrapers. A windshield wiper serves as a bow. The Chevy and I are guest soloist.

The crowd parts to allow Frieda through. She walks royally, each step as if trying to throw off a shoe.

She takes her place in front of the musicians, clears her throat, raises an oil dipstick . . .

The prelude begins slowly, processionally. A B note (Buick Roadmaster, 1956), an E (Dynamic 88, 1960s), the Buick again,

three successive G sharps from a Studebaker Hawk. Then, Frieda cues me. I press the Chevy's horn, and for once my automobile is saying something besides, "Out of my way, jerk!" It is helping to tell an ageless story, one these people never tire of hearing. Then the room fills with an icy, swarming vibrato; hornets riding in on a storm cloud. It is the sound of the frusenstogens; you feel it along your spine, like the windchill factor.

.   .   .

The audience loves the overture. They give Frieda an ovation. I guess they like me, too. They slap me on the back as they
drift out. Someone tells me to stop by the bakery for complimentary pfeffernusse. The only bad review is from an eighty-year-old
guy asleep on a mechanic's creeper.

Frieda can't help reaching in and pushing the Chevy's
horn.

"Perfect pitch!" she keeps gushing, and every time she
smiles, her face shatters into Safety Glass.

"Take the car," I hear myself saying. What the hell. I can't
afford gas anyway.

And there's no more Platformate around.

.   .   .

So if you are ever approaching little Faust, North Carolina,
and hear what sounds like a traffic jam in the distance—listen
closely. It is the sound of Frieda Mallinkrodt's Complete Texaco
Tannhäuser Orchestra.

I have an honorary seat there.

SOAP FOR ONE

KEEZLETOWN, TENNESSEE.

After I give up the Chevy, there is nothing to do but rely on others for transportation. But I will not solicit. I will walk, always moving, shuffling, churning toward some new destination, so that people sensing my determination will be compelled to offer a lift.

I develop a style. Loose-jointed, ambiant, flappy—but with a dogged eyes-forward visage.

"He looked fixated," people might say if asked to describe me in passing. "He was hardnosin' the highway."

"At least his clothes looked clean."

. . .

Ah, to have a Laundromat to oneself for the night! There just aren't enough hours to do everything.

First, I stand out front letting it blow its hot square of breath over me. The doors are wide open. There are no locks. The Laundromat never closes.

Inside the air is moist and coastal, charged with possibility. On one wall there are only a few boldfaced restrictions, so I memorize them:

<u>NO</u> Tinting
<u>NO</u> Dyeing
<u>NO</u> Rubberized Articles
<u>NO</u> Rugs

And a handwritten addendum:

<u>NO</u> Pup-Tents

I play the change machine for a while, turning dollars to quarters, quarters to nickels and dimes, nickels and dimes back to quarters. After an hour I'm still even. Better odds than Vegas.

The individual soaps peer out from periscope windows, and I put in a quarter and crank one out. The box is hard and compact and exudes a confidence of form. Someone, some-where, is making a nice little profit off of Loneliness in America.

I pay ten cents for a plastic laundry bag, punch out arm holes and a neck, and pad around in it while my clothes wash. In the dryer window it looks like a patent-leather hospital gown. I wait for the washer to hit "soak," and when it does, I buy myself a Coke, lower the lights, and dance to the Maytag rhumba.

· · ·

"FILL DIRT WANTED" reads an index card on the bul-letin board. I dial the number.
"Hello?"
"Hi. I hear you're looking for some dirt."
"Not at three in the morning. [Pause.] What kind of dirt?"
"Well I don't actually have any, but I seem to recall seeing quite a lot of it on the way into town."
"Why are you calling?"
"I was just curious why you would want dirt."
"I like dirt. What about it?"
Apparently, Keezletown is rife with pets. There are rabbits for sale, kittens for sale, gerbils for sale, free German shepherds to good homes, parakeets, live minnows. One sign reads simply:

AKC FOR SALE. ALL PAPERS.

Someone named Greta has lost a Great Dane who answers to Vidor.
Another card, same handwriting, reads:

I WILL BABYSIT YOUR CHILDREN IN MY HOME. GRETA

Who would trust their kids to Greta, I think to myself.

· · ·

I put the clothes in the dryer, walk over to the magazine table. There are *Look*s and *Life*s from the 60s. The *Reader's Digest*, with its exposed contents flap, looks like a man who wears his vest outside his suit: "Humor in Uniform," "Life in These United States," "The Fluoride Fallacy" by Dr. Erund Novak, "I Am Joe's Endocrine Gland" (the series was running out of body parts). In a *Saturday Evening Post* (1962) I read the account of John Glenn's *Friendship-7* flight. The photos leap from the page in brilliant reds and yellows. America was never seen in a more rarified light, and in a burst of patriotic fervor I climb inside the Sudzy-Boy Heavy-Duty Washer and reenact the historic splashdown, emerging to the tumbling fanfare of a dryer. Then, exhausted, I stretch out on the laundry-folding table and sleep.

· · ·

I awake at dawn aware of being watched. There is a face at the window. Squarish, almost mythological.

It is Vidor.

I pull my clothes from the dryer and dress and step out in the Tennessee dawn. The Great Dane is gone. I walk through Keezletown out towards the bypass, keep walking, eyes ahead, waiting for someone to offer a lift.

· · ·

"At least his clothes look clean," they might say in passing.

SPAP-OOP

ENID, OKLAHOMA.

People say Mom & Pop stores are disappearing. Don't tell that to Pandi Neeb.

"Friendliness is my most important product!" he shouts as I enter. I ask him where the Vienna sausages are.

"That's a smart food," he says. "A Vienna sausage knows where it's from. Like the brussels sprout."

We split a can of sausages and he tells me about his native Pakistan.

"Pakistan was born in 1947. And it has been fighting ever since. Baluchistan fights the Punjabis who fight the Sindhis and the Pushtuns. I realize this means nothing to you, but it is like if Oklahoma and Arkansas and Missouri and Kansas were at war with each other. So, for my family's safety, we moved to America. I bought this store from a retired couple. My wife raises the kids and still weaves carpets at night. And we live in a Gold Medallion Home."

Pandi is teaching himself to read.

"Everything I learned, I learned from stocking these shelves. This store is my library! Only in America are there so many happy products."

He points out some of his happy products. *Viva. Bounce. Payday Bars.*

A little girl comes in.

"Can I have a Slurpee, please?"

"You certainly can. Would you like a carpet with that?"

"No, thank you. Just a Slurpee."

Most of the customers know him by name.

"Hey, Pandi, you got any blackeye peas!?"

"Vegetables always sound injured," he says. "Squash. Artichokes. Beets."

I never thought about that. One thing I noticed is that a lot of Pandi's products are upside down.

Some stores have *M&M*s. Pandi has *W&W*s.

I tell him about a commercial I used to watch. Before color.

Two Ms were sitting beside a pool, soaking up rays. One was a plain M, very proper. The other was a peanut M from Dixie. Big and loud. You always sort of thought those guys were gonna get into a fight, but they discovered they had something in common:

"We melt in your mouth. Not in your hand."

Exactly what mothers wanted to hear. They were a couple of good salesmen.

Pandi likes my story.

"Someday, our provinces will live like those *M&M*s. Then I will go home. But for now, I like America."

And at 11:00 he locks up his little store full of Zest and Pride and Ho-Hos. He heads off toward his Gold Medallion Home. I stand in the parking lot. There are some new apartments going up across the street from this little country store. I'm not crazy about seeing that. But I like the sign:

IF YOU LIVED HERE YOU'D BE HOME BY NOW

THE POSEIDON PARTY

AUSTIN, TEXAS.

It is 10:00 in the morning and I am having breakfast at a Chili Parlor on 6th Street. Two tables over, a fierce-looking guy wears a T-shirt that reads, "Linoleum Cutters Do It on the Floor." I bite into a yellow pepper. With a kind of soft "pock!", it explodes, shooting tiny seeds into his eye. He howls, as if maimed for life, and rises, his eye already swimming in red. He has a carpet knife in his hand. I back out the door, playing to his blind side.

Violence happens that fast in Texas. A small "pock!", and someone is trying to turn you into small pieces of Congoleum.

I walk along 6th Street where in the unobstructed distance the U. of T. tower rises like a carbine shell. Every alley on 6th Street blows a beery morning breath into my face.

I try to hitch out of Austin, but the only offers come from David Crosby look-alikes: guys with pistols on the seat and powdered doughnut on their nose. I walk south along I-35. The exit ramps are full of forlorn hitchhikers. One, dressed in camouflage, stands against a grassy embankment wondering why he hasn't got a ride in four days. Mistletoe sits in the trees like cannonballs.

I turn east along Route 71, keep walking, and soon the medians become furred with bluebonnets and Indian paintbrush.

Austin is now in the distance though the tower is still clearly visible, still close enough for the Ghost of Charles Whitman to squint and say, "I can get him from here. . . ."

•   •   •

"Forget about Austin," says Naydra Zundorf, fine-tuning Moe Bandy on the radio. We are in the cab of her Hot Wagon, pulling a gleaming carapace of Stewart sandwiches, Slim Jim's, Snappy Tom, Penrose sausages.

"Forget Houston, Forget Dallas. This . . ." she says, extending an upturned hand out the window as if serving Bastrop on a platter, "is the most peaceful town in Texas. And the only one ain't ruined in some way. Austin is supposed to be a real artsy-craftsy place now, you know. Cultured. And it has Lake Travis. My boyfriend keeps a pencil-boat there. But there's always that—"

"Tower," I finish.

"Right." She breaks into an obscure lyric. " 'Oh, there was a rumor 'bout a tumor . . .' That's from 'The Ballad of Charles Whitman,' " she says. "They actually played that on the radio *a lot.*"

She pronounces "a lot" with a gleeful exaggeration. As if it were a self-invented catchphrase.

"Or take the Big D. There's money there. And folks are friendly enough. But then you stand down at Dealey Plaza and realize *the worst thing that ever happened to America happened in Dallas.* As for Houston, well . . . highest unreported murder rate in the nation."

I wonder how a statistic like that gets unearthed.

Naydra wears a denim studded jacket. The studs resemble hundreds of small bullets.

She pulls the truck into a construction site: *Lake Bastrop Estates. Carefree Living from $40,000.*

"Know what used to be here?"

"What?"

"A German PW camp. Rommel's soldiers were interned here. The first thing they saw on the dining tables was raisin bread. They laughed out loud. Whoever heard of putting raisins in bread! A few years later, when the war ended, practically every one of them stayed in Bastrop. Including my dad."

Naydra blows the Klaghorn. Workers turn, drop lumber, peppily approach the truck. Many of them carry small vinyl cases.

•   •   •

All along the Sun Belt housing is up. Naydra's Hot Wagon soaks in the rays of success, a shimmering aluminum quilt. But most of that success is due to her own entrepreneurial vision.

"It was just one of those ideas that walks up and taps you on the shoulder," says Naydra. "At first I thought it sounded crazy." She smiles. "But then, so did raisin bread, didn't it?"

A man steps up.

"Hi, Tubo," says Naydra. Tubo is a carpenter. He wears his hammer slung low, Eastwood style.

"I wanna extend this for one more day," he says, holding out a copy of *Thunderbolt and Lightfoot.*

"Sure. What else?"

"Sausage biscuit."

Naydra unwraps a biscuit, thumbs it apart as if shuffling a deck of cards, whisks it into a microwave; pushes—without looking—several numbered squares: a flurry of precision.

She wheels and deals.

"Now, Tubo, if you liked this I have *Heaven's Gate* by the same director. It cost forty-two million, but I can let you have it for a dollar-fifty a day."

The sausage biscuit emerges hot and damp, a puffy suspect: food cooked fast forward.

"Who's next?"

"You got *Rambo* on Beta?"

"Still out."

"Damn. Then gimme *Cartoon Festival #4.*"

Lucien Hatch steps up. Lucien is a roofer, you can see where the sun has bounced off the flashing and burned the underside of his chin, his nose, and his eyelids, giving him an upside-down sunburn.

He fans his nail apron impatiently.

"So hell, Naydra, is it here or not!!"

Naydra scans the tape selection.

"It's here."

"H'awllright!" Lucien turns and announces to everyone in earshot.

"Listen up ya'll!! . . . Poseidon Party! Tonight! My place!!"
He looks at me.
"This a friend of yours, Nay?"
"Yeah."
"Then bring him along."

•　　•　　•

Texas' history is steeped in violence. The Alamo, the Bowie
knife, the buffalo slaughter, the Comanche slaughter. The southern part of the state is a knife in Mexico's shoulders, the north-
ern part a boxer's illegal thumb jabbing at Oklahoma. In between are the birthplaces or bodies of John Wesley Hardin,
Clyde Barrow, Dean Corll, Baby Face Nelson . . .
The Sesquicentennial isn't coming off as big a hoot as
hoped. No one can quite pronounce it ("sequelcentennial,"
"sasquatchcentennial") and it's fifty-nine years behind the rest of
the nation. Texas doesn't like to trail anyone.

•　　•　　•

Twenty-two people show up for Lucien's Poseidon Party,
Naydra and I, Tubo, and most of the construction crew. Lucien's
living room has been paneled in hoarded cedar. Texas Cavalry
swords line one wall. The guests gather around the television
whose legs stick straight up like a dead click beetle.
They have each paid a dollar to watch *The Poseidon Ad-
venture* upside down.
Lucien will use the money to make his monthly VCR
payment to Montgomery Ward.
He keeps replaying the capsize scene. Passengers float
spectrally upward, the furniture sticks to the floor, Shelley Win-
ters thrashes about in a Christmas tree. In each frozen frame
there is a joyous newfound quirk of gravity.
All through the party, I keep waiting for one of those Texas-
style brawls to break out, the ones you always hear about at

places like Billy Bob's in Ft. Worth. But at 11:00 p.m. Naydra looks at her watch and says she has to go free the babysitter.

"You can stay here or you can stay at my house," she says.

I go with her. I'm sure these partyers are secretly waiting for me to leave so they can take down those swords and really go at it.

·   ·   ·

Violence breaks out in the Most Peaceful Town in Texas the next morning. It is swift and sudden. Naydra's three boys are working in the front yard. The oldest is stacking branches in a wagon. The two younger ones linger near a live oak, conspiring. One sneaks up behind the oldest boy, plants himself on all fours.

The other circles, makes some small talk and "pock!", shoves him in the chest. But the attack is overstaged and somehow all three end up in a sprawling, giggling clot on the ground.

I get out of Bastrop. Things are getting ugly.

SHOE IN THE ROAD

You can learn a lot about America by keeping your head to the ground.

In my travels I have discovered that, on any given stretch of road, the three most common objects you are likely to come across are:

1. A large chunk of tire.
2. Those plastic gaskets that hold six-packs together.
3. A shoe.

Yes, a shoe. Always alone. Never in pairs.

This happens so often it's astounding. I used to stand there and examine the shoe and try to imagine what series of events could have led to this. The more I would think about it, the more improbable the whole thing would seem.

How does someone lose a perfectly good shoe?

I started asking around.

"Kids will steal anything," says Carl Hufnagle, forty-eight, who has run Hufnagles on Main for twenty-six years.

He turns the shoe over in his hands, inspecting it for damage. I had come across it on Highway 51, south of town. A new snakeskin high heel, 6½D. No scuffs. No crinkles.

"See, we like to display one of each of our styles on a rack in front of the store, where people can pick 'em up and examine 'em. Put their nose right up there to the quality.

"Occasionally some kid—some unsupervised type—will come along and steal one, just because it's there. Just for kicks. Later, maybe he'll be out riding with his friends and show it around. You know, bragging. His friends will say 'Great, now what are you gonna *do* with it?' And the kid will think about that and just chuck it out the window. Happens all the time."

He thanks me and adds:

"It's not all the kids. Just a few."

"Of course."

"You weren't expecting any kind of reward were you?"

He nods to a male customer entering, follows him inside.

I watch him seat the customer, straddle a miniature sliding board, and begin unlacing the man's shoe.

Total service.

•   •   •

Along a newly repaved stretch of New Mexico highway I find a construction workboot, size 8D. The steel toe is bent.

A few miles ahead I come across a DOT crew.

Kenny Diehl is lurking behind a pickup truck, reorganizing tools—a look-busy project. He would rather not have the crew foreman see that he is wearing one 8D and one 16EEE boot.

"What happened?" I ask, returning his other boot.

"I dropped a fifty gallon drum of creosote. Some buddies helped me get my boot off and ran me out to the clinic and back." He studies the returned boot.

"Guess I left this behind." He limps toward the cab and tosses the boot in.

"Shouldn't you be laid up?" I ask.

He points toward the site trailer where a black and yellow sign boasts:

1,130 DAYS WITHOUT A LOST TIME ACCIDENT

"Would you wanna be the horse's ass?" he says.

• • •

Once, in Iowa, I began collecting a shoe every hundred yards or so. A brogan. A golf shoe. A Corfam (space-age vinyl 1968–1969) casual. It began to look like some bizarre practical joke. Until I reached a motel outside of Flat Rapids.

I had to knock several times before the door opened.

"What!!"

"Hi there. I came across some mementos of yours."

He slammed the door. Not a good time.

I left the shoes outside his room. Someday he might want to have them bronzed or something.

·   ·   ·

Some other observations:

You find a lot of discarded shoes near rest stops. This is because people step in animal crap at rest stops. When they climb back in the car, the owner makes them throw the shoe out rather than put up with the smell.

On the last day of school, a kid will be walking home carrying his gym shoes. They will be smelly and covered with ink pictographs. He will realize he no longer has any need for the shoes and hurl them over a telephone wire. Gravity and nature will eventually return them to earth, one at a time. This happens all over the country in the last week of May. If you find a sneaker or basketball shoe, look up. You will probably see its partner dangling.

·   ·   ·

When I find a small Buster Brown dress shoe near an elementary school, I can easily picture its young owner hobbling about the hallways, hapless and ridiculed. I take the shoe to the principal's office.

The secretary seems concerned.

"If anyone lost a shoe, please report to the Lost and Found," she announces over the PA.

Roughly two-thirds of the student body shows up.

Naturally, a few are taking advantage of a wide open opportunity to get out of class. But oddly enough, most have at some point in the school year lost a shoe. Next time you watch a cluster of kids board a school bus, keep your eye on the last kid. It is a secret, gleeful practice of schoolbus drivers to close the hydraulic door too quickly and clip off a shoe.

If you find a kid's shoe on the highway, leave it there. Someone will probably be by at 3:30 to pick it up.

THE GOOD GUY

TEXAS PANHANDLE.

"I don't wear this thing everyday," says Hugh McManaway, pushing a gigantic foam rubber cowboy hat out of his face.

"Only on the days I'm a Good Guy."

We are driving along Highway 520, which is barren and black, and nailed to the earth by telephone poles.

Besides the hat, Hugh is wearing a dark business suit and hiking boots.

"Spent all day appraising some farm property over in Dalhart. Most people think all a savings and loan officer does is shuffle paper and give away calendars, but you got to go out and examine every property before you give the OK. You got to inspect the house and grounds and walk off the dimensions.

"Now this place up in Dalhart, hell, it was deeded in 1843, before surveys. The boundary markers are all natural landmarks: trees and boulders and what all. So the deed actually reads: "Bordered on the south by a creek."

"What most folks don't realize is, over the years a creek can shift. Sometimes hundreds of yards. The couple buying this place in Dalhart—they think they're gettin' 25 acres, but it's actually closer to 30."

He grins.

"So, today I'm a Good Guy. I approved those folks' loan."

Hugh's car is a 1969 Pontiac Bonneville, a low Jurassic creature with a deceptively powerful engine. In the distance, framed against bruised squatting clouds, is the skyline of Detroit: the turreted Renaissance Center, the Westin Hotel. Later this will turn out to be a massive granary.

Hugh studies his watch and guns the vehicle to seventy.

"I wanna get to The Cattlemans before it closes," he explains.

All along Texas 520 are billboards for The Cattlemans:

HURRY TO THE CATTLEMANS! HOME OF THE 72 OZ. STEAK. EAT IT ALL AND YOU DON'T PAY!!

The billboard features a four-pound steak lapping over the edge of the platter. It is shaped, vaguely, like Texas itself.

EAT IT ALL AND YOU DON'T PAY!

When travelers see the billboard, they floor it for The Cattlemans.

And behind every one of those billboards lurks a State Trooper.

By the time most travelers reach The Cattlemans they have already collected a thirty-dollar speeding ticket. Furthermore, they usually end up paying full price for the meal, since, in addition to the seventy-two ounce steak, you have to consume a hassock-size potato and a quarter acre of tossed salad.

Hugh's appetite is as big as his hat.

We barrel along at seventy-five, eighty, eighty-five. He isn't worried about State Troopers. Instead, he furiously scans the side of the road. Suddenly he whips the car over to a halt, bolts

out and chases something through the dirt. When he comes back his breath is short and he throws a boxer's shrug of bravado. His fist is clinched tightly.

"Caught me a ticket repellent," he says, winking.

When we hit sixty-five, Hugh reaches out and applies the ticket repellent to the windshield:

A grayish lizard about seven inches long. Velocity holds it in place.

"Table for two coming up," grins Hugh, and guns the car toward The Cattlemans.

•   •   •

We are pulled over by a State Trooper ten miles from the steakhouse. It is, of course, inevitable.

The lizard is still on the windshield. Frozen in place by fear.

Hugh's explanation is reasonable.

"Sorry, officer. I had to speed up to blow this thing off my windshield. It's obstructing my vision."

The trooper studies the reptile for a moment, then gingerly removes it from the windshield. He sets it in the dirt beside the pavement.

"Just drive carefully," he says, and returns to his car, shaking his head.

We make it to The Cattlemans five minutes before closing.

Most of the diners emerge dyspeptically, but in a few there is the clear waddle of victory. Men roll toothpicks in their teeth and parade their stomachs across the parking lot the way a coach parades his star athlete.

Inside, Hugh takes his time, savoring every bite. Waitresses glower and a busboy stacks chairs around us making a roomful of antlers.

He finishes every morsel, pays for mine, though I protest.

"Forget it. Ain't nothin'," replies the Good Guy. "Hell, I already gave away five acres today."

A FINE SIGHT TO SEE

ARIZONA.

There are a million things to do in Arizona.

You can visit the Painted Desert and watch the pastel landscape shifting hues hourly. You can descend by burro or helicopter into the Grand Canyon, or raft on the Colorado.

You can stand in Arizona and three other states at the same time.

You can see the London Bridge in Lake Havasu or you can surf in Tempe.

I didn't do any of that.

But I did stand on a corner in Winslow, Arizona.

And it was a fine sight to see.

No one can explain why, but Winslow is crawling with beautiful girls, and to meet them, all you have to do is stand on the corner. In no time a truck (usually a flatbed Ford) will slow down and a stunning blonde or redhead will be giving you the once over.

⋅ ⋅ ⋅

"Hey, handsome, climb on up here."

Is she talking to me? My hair is brittle and matted from the sun. There are tree rings of sweat under my arms. *Could* she be talking to me?

"Yeah, you, maverick."

I climb in. She is wearing turquoise and Tony Llamas. She reaches over and buckles me in.

"All snug?"

And we cruise along the main drag. A flatbed truck weighs close to four and a half tons, and you can fit a pair of Datsuns on the back of one, but the girls here seem to prefer them.

When she lets me out, a redhead is waiting to pick me up. And a brunette after that.

It's just a fine sight to see.

•   •   •

Jackson Browne wrote a song about Winslow, Arizona, in 1972. It was called "Take It Easy."

•   •   •

"I was the inspiration for that song," says Samantha, who smells of desert lilac. "He was standing on that corner right there. I gave him a ride."

We are driving around Winslow, counting Ford truck dealerships. So far I've counted thirty-six.

"What was he like?"

"Quiet. Kind of depressed."

"Yeah. I've heard that about him."

•   •   •

When Jackson got back to California, he told his friends, the Eagles, about the town with the flatbed-driving women.

"I swear up and down," he said to the Eagles, "Just stand on the corner."

The Eagles went to Winslow, Arizona, and stood on the corner.

Sure enough, a fleet of flatbeds quickly appeared honking and waving. The Eagles went home and recorded the song that became a huge, huge hit.

And, for a brief while, Winslow was the Pride of Arizona.

Thousands flocked there. Cowboys, scholars, servicemen, frat brothers, grifters, drifters, rounders; married men stashed their wives in RVs, and then sneaked off to the famous corner to see if it was true what they said. . . .

Someone introduced a bill to make "Take It Easy" the state song, and on license plates that year the slogan "Grand Canyon State" was replaced by "Come on baby, don't say maybe."

But as the song faded, so did the tourism. The Jackson Browne Motel is now boarded up. The Eagles statue was dismantled when the band added personnel.

But you can still stand on the corner in Winslow, Arizona, and pretty soon a large truck will rumble up beside you, and a stunning, statuesque figure will laugh and ask how far you're going. . . .

You may lose or you may win . . .
But you will never be there again . . .
It's a fine sight to see.

DROP IN ANY MAILBOX

MORRO BAY, CALIFORNIA.

Simpson's Motel sits on the "old highway," flexing its neon, as if to say to the interstate a mile or so away, "Hey, I'm still here." At the counter, I have to ring twice. Simpson emerges from a small, dark room. I can barely make out a daybed and a flickering TV.

"Sorry. I was watching *The Big Valley.*

He gives me a key. Room 12. Written on the key is an astonishing guarantee:

DROP IN ANY MAILBOX. WE GUARANTEE POSTAGE.

I walk to my room. There is an ice machine outside the door. The bathroom is early Chiclet.

It's only 9:30, so I go back to the office and try to strike up a conversation with Simpson.

"Weirdest thing caught on a few years back," he says. "Local families would come in here and rent a room just to watch cable."

Actually, I'm more interested in the key.

"Can I really drop this in any mailbox?"

"The weekend we showed *On Golden Pond,* we were full up."

Abruptly, he says, "Bedtime," snaps off the office lights and recedes into the flickering gray.

Walking back to my room I wonder if there's a special branch of the Post Office that does nothing but return motel keys. Everything is awash in soft pulsating neon. Pink. Green. Pink. Green. Outside my door, the ice machine rattles dice. Through the wall I hear a screaming couple, muffled threats, the sound of lumber splitting, a child bawling in fright, television surf, doors slamming.

It is too noisy to sleep.

So I decide to sit up all night.

No one ever sits up all night at a motel. You like to get in as much sleep as possible, and in the morning calculate the hours to see if you got your money's worth.

But the ice machine is relentless and the people next door are rehearsing a Sam Shephard play, so I take a seat in a chair by the flameproof curtains and watch the cadence of pastel light in the parking lot.

Around 3 a.m., the first of several dozen mailmen arrive. By four they are everywhere.

There are mailmen in the pool.

Mailmen perched on the railing, quaffing beer. Mailmen playing shuffleboard. They seem to be having the time of their lives.

I decide to join them.

"We weren't keeping you awake, were we?" one asks, concerned.

"No. I'm staying up all night."

"Come on in. We were getting ready to do some trolling."

The rooms have waterbeds *and* Magic Fingers. Five of us climb aboard and start it up. The effect is very much like an electric bass boat.

Around 5:00, everyone settles down to take in a viewing of *Blame It on Rio*. Then they cover their tracks, pocket the keys, and sneak off into the dawn.

•   •   •

Back in my room, the door opens with a tentative creek. The Gideon Man lets himself in, turns, and sees me awake. I never see his key though the door is locked.

"Didn't expect to see anyone up at this hour," he whispers.

He wears crepe-soled shoes.

He crosses to the dresser, opens the bottom drawer, disappointed to see a Bible still there.

"Feel free to steal this," he says waving the Bible at me.

He pulls a handful of cards from his shirt and thoughtfully selects one.

"Here." His voice never rises above a whisper.

The card features a biblical verse and shows an address for The Gideons in Bakersfield, California.

"If you're ever through, stop by."

"I will, I promise."

"Be careful. It's in a bad part of town. We sort of encourage break-in's.

"Well," he says as he shoulders the box of Bibles, "on-ward."

He floats out, somehow locking the door behind him.

·   ·   ·

I once stayed at a hotel in New York City that cost one hundred and seventy-five dollars a night. The clothes hangers were lopped off at the neck to keep people from stealing them. At Simpson's Motel the coat hangers are free. I sent a dozen to my friend Ahmed, the whiplash victim.

CHARLEY

BIGGS, OREGON.

The highway around Biggs looks like a Jackson Pollock painting. Rivulets of tar on a canvas of Portland cement.

The highway is full of cracks. Once a month the highway department comes along and fills in the cracks with tar. Then someone comes along and squeezes the tar out again like toothpaste.

That someone is Charley Scarborough.

Every month Charley delivers 23,000 pounds of new cars from the GM plant in Orion, Michigan, to Seattle. Never once does his truck touch Interstate.

He drives by night.

"I found my own route," he explains. "No tolls. No weigh stations. I know every back road between here and Lake Michigan. Every low overhang that ain't as low as it says it is. I save six hundred dollars every haul."

"Sounds like you got a Short-Hop Suspension," I say.

The road gives our words vibrato. For the last forty miles, it has been one zipper of tar.

He turns up the Four Tops on the custom Kenwood, but the ratcheting beneath the wheels makes their voices sound like bagpipes.

Suddenly the music dies. The headlights go out. The truck is plunged into blackness.

Charley flips some switches, studies the amp gauge.

"Must've rubbed some wiring raw," he says and squints, trying to navigate by moonlight.

"Shouldn't we stop?" I ask as the semi rafts dangerously from one side of the road to the other.

"No truckstops for miles. There's nothing out there but volcano ash."

Trees, poles, fence rails appear to be backing toward us.

A pair of taillights comet out of the black and Charley has to slam the air brakes. He leans forward, cradling the steering wheel and biting his lip, checks his watch, and says:

"Tell you what. Whynchoo climb up to the top car up there and switch on the high-beams."

Minutes later I am sitting in luxury high above the highway, getting unbelievable mileage. The headlights throw down a pool of light that Charley's cab chases. At one point he pulls over and calls out, "Are you playin' the radio?"

"It sounds great! I got the moonroof open."

"*Don't fiddle with anything!* You're draining the battery! Those lights have to last."

Somewhere in the deep a.m. an old DeSoto plays into view ahead of us. As it creeps along, its fins begin to wobble and then the car dives off the road, spinning a maelstrom of dust and gravel. It ends up in a field, one headlight sunk in ash.

Charley stops the truck and climbs out. I drop down, and we jog back toward the DeSoto.

The driver is sitting on the rear of the DeSoto furiously smoking a cigarette, muttering.

"You okay?" asks Charley.

"I'm still here, ain't I?" he answers.

"Sorry. Didn't mean to scare you."

"Nothing scares me. But when I looked behind me and saw those lights shining down I thought to myself, 'If that truck's

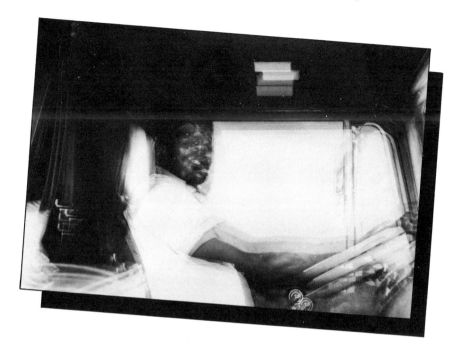

half as wide as it is tall, I'd better get the hell off the road.'"

We push the DeSoto out of the field. The driver thanks us guardedly and pulls away in reverse, as if trying to back out of a bad dream.

THE P & C MAN

WHATCOM COUNTY, WASHINGTON.

It's not easy asking redemption for 106,000 county residents.

It's not easy making them all laugh either.

But day in, day out, five days a week, Trip Ware has to do it.

Trip has two of the toughest jobs in journalism.

He's the Daily Prayer & Daily Chuckle editor for the Whatcom County *Daily Herald.*

"It's thankless, creditless work," says Trip, working on coffee number four of the morning. "You get no byline, two postage stamps of space to work with. . . ."

"So why do you do it?"

"Because I'm a staple. For twenty-two years folks have picked up the *Daily Herald* and right there, mixed in with all the depressing stuff, are two little outposts of Humanity. Right now I'm working on the Prayer. Then, I have a little lunch, I come back, I write the Chuckle. It's a monumental shift of themes, and frankly it can make you a little schizo."

We are crouched in his tiny office in the basement of the *Daily Herald.* (Prayer & Chuckle men always get the runtiest

office.) Shelves and sills are crammed with an eclectic mix: theological tracts mingled with the works of Orben, Cerf, Joey Adams; an outcropping of *The Upper Room* between the pages of *1001 Quips and Rejoinders for All Occasions.*

Trip gets up, looks out the window at a pair of passing feet, sits, rises again, slugs back some coffee, and glares at the typewriter.

"I'm having trouble getting an angle this morning."

I look at what he has written so far:

AMEN

"I always try to get my ending first, then work backwards," he explains.

"Good idea."

It is a Friday. From what I've seen, Whatcom County can get pretty woolly on weekends. I mention this to Trip.

"What're you suggesting? A sort of Blanket Repentance?"

"Yeah. Something that absolves everybody for everything for the whole weekend."

He thinks about this a moment.

"That's *awfully* commercial . . ."

But soon his Smith-Corona hums. I sit by quietly, self-consciously, at one point starting to leave.

"No, no, no, no . . . stay!" he insists, not looking up. "It's good to have a warm body in the room, just to bounce ideas off of."

·   ·   ·

He whips the paper from the typewriter, thrusts it at me triumphantly.

"Whaddya think? Be honest."

I read it:

DEAR GOD IN HEAVEN, FORGIVE US OUR TRANSGRESSIONS AND TEACH US TO WALK IN THE PATH OF THY LIGHT. AMEN.

"It's good," I say. "It's tight, economical writing."

He takes it back, scans it once more, nods in self-approval and underhands it to a passing copyboy who will proofread it and verify the names and addresses.

"One down. . . ." says Trip Ware.

·   ·   ·

Lunch at the Biscuit Bucket. Trip scarfs down two sausage biscuits and an iced tea, the flush of creativity still on his face.

A shy waitress refills his glass at least a half-dozen times. Finally she gets up the nerve to speak.

"I really . . . like your work. . . ." she blurts, hurrying away.

Trip smiles and leaves a dollar tip. Byline or no byline, people in Whatcom County know Trip Ware.

· · ·

1:30. It is half an hour to the *Herald*'s "bedtime," and Trip is still wrestling with the Chuckle, circling, trying to sneak up on an idea.

All afternoon has been toying with a drunk joke, which links thematically with the prayer.

Fishing for encouragement, he shows me what he's written so far:

ONE DRUNK TO ANOTHER

"Those are likeable characters," I say. "You really wanna get to know them."

"I don't know. Maybe I should change it to 'lush.' Else there'll be flak from the MADD Mothers. Drunks drive. Lushes stay at the bar."

He fires off a quick rewrite:

ONE LUSH TO ANOTHER

"I just don't know what happens next," he says, falling silent.

We both think for a while.

"A colon," I suggest finally.

He looks at me, then at the page.

"Yeah . . . yeah . . . that'll work." He nods. ". . . that'll work."

And he types a rapid burst:

ONE LUSH TO ANOTHER:

•   •   •   '

2:00. The Editor-in-Chief's office. Trip is fidgeting, dismantling a Styrofoam coffee cup. The cloud of rejection is something he must deal with every working day of his life.   ,

The Editor-in-Chief reads the Chuckle, having already finished the Prayer, the order readers usually follow. His face acknowledges nothing, not even Trip's sure hand for dialogue:

ONE LUSH TO ANOTHER:
I DON'T HAVE A DRINKING PROBLEM.
I GET DRUNK, I FALL OFF THE
STOOL, NO PROBLEM.

The Chief looks up, taking his time.
"Front-page stuff," he announces. "Both of 'em."
And Trip can't help but break into a grin.
You'd think he'd be a little more jaded.
After all, for twenty-two years a Trip Ware Daily Prayer &
Daily Chuckle have never failed to make the front page.

•   •   •

These are some of the afternoon papers that went under recently.

THE MEMPHIS PRESS-SCIMITAR
THE CLEVELAND PRESS
THE PHILADELPHIA BULLETIN
THE CHARLOTTE NEWS
THE WINSTON-SALEM SENTINEL
MY HOMETOWN PAPER

Some of them got killed in afternoon traffic, trying to be delivered. Others just couldn't compete with the morning papers.

It seems like no one takes the afternoon paper seriously. People like their news hard, with coffee, first thing in the morning. Or in the evening from a stern authoritarian. A Peter Jennings. A Tom Brokaw.

But I wonder if David Brinkley used to come home after his broadcast . . . when there still was a *Washington Star* . . . open it up and start right in on the Jumblets. . . .

Maybe Sam Donaldson turned to the Pigskin Pick-it.

There is much more to a newspaper than news. There is the backhanded optimism of the obituaries. (For every one person who dies it lists at least a dozen still surviving.) There is the Wednesday Food Section—the papers' fat suit, maybe—but a small town pivots on those coupons and recipes and canning tips. Kids read the school lunch menu and steel themselves. There is Art.

Who hasn't spent entire afternoons immersed in the flawless imperfections of a Find-Six-Things-Wrong-With-This-Picture? I know I have.

There is Science. "Ask Andy" to explain the Doppler Effect and he'll not only comply, he'll toss in a set of Encyclopedias.

There is Poetry in the wedding announcements. Searing, transcendent passages:

THE COUPLE PLAN TO HONEYMOON
IN LAKE HAVASU BEFORE RETURNING
TO BLAINE WHERE THE HUSBAND
DRIVES A SNAP-ON TRUCK.

Maybe afternoon papers *are* vanishing. Tell that to Trip Ware. He'll tell you things are just fine at the Whatcom County *Daily Herald*. He'll tell you it's the big city papers that haven't got a Prayer. Or a Chuckle.

5¢ to a Dollar

POCATELLO, IDAHO.

One dollar.

I have decided to see if it's still possible to get a decent meal for a dollar. My quest is now into its second day. I'm pretty damn hungry. Leaning against the window of Edna's Egg Nook, I peer inside. I can see a pile of discarded oranges next to the juice machine. They have been turned inside out, squeezed of every drop of vitality. That's how I feel.

"What can I get for a dollar?" I ask at the register.

"You can get eighteen silver-dollar pancakes."

I know better. Silver-dollar pancakes are nothing more than tiny satellites that form around real pancakes.

I try the Family Steak House.

"What can I get for a dollar?"

"The salad bar," says a hostess in gingham. She motions toward a bin where vegetables sweat beneath a pair of sauna lamps. A sheet of Plexiglas keeps them just beyond arm's length.

When you're starving you hear things.

"You can get half a calf," I think I hear the counterman at the Health Hut say.

"Sounds great!! I'll take it!"

What he'd said was "half-and-half," a vegetable-soybean patty on Hunza bread. I slink away.

I find the Dollar Meal at the 5¢ to $1.00 store.

66

The store has a special at the Luncheonette counter: Banana splits 5¢ to $1.00. There is a cluster of balloons floating above the register. Inside each balloon is a carefully folded piece of paper. The price of the banana split is written on that paper. Now, I'm no gambling man, but it seems to me that this is an offer with better than winnable odds.

The balloons bob and turn on a rotisserie of air. They seem to be mocking me. I consider every nuance of color and placement. Why, for instance, is there only one yellow balloon? Why does that red one float so conspicuously apart from the others?

The waitress is reading a cosmetology handbook, maybe planning a career jump. She catches me staring at her and averts her eyes. I turn back to the balloons.

If there is a 5¢ balloon, I decide, it is probably buried in the middle somewhere.

The waitress rises, begins chopping celery. It is Tuesday. Tuna Special Day.

Among the cluster of balloons are several dark green ones. They seem to hint of self-concealment.

"I've made my choice," I announce.

The waitress guides a few bits of celery off the edge of her knife, then turns and approaches me. "Wanda," her name tag reads.

I point to the centermost green.

"That one right there."

"This one?" she asks. Her knife flashes upwards.

Pop.

We stare at the little green sausage end. She has popped the wrong balloon.

"Not that green one. *That* green one."

"Sorry," she mutters, casually opens the folded slip, studies it.

"Sure you don't want this one?" she says. Her voice is like a zipper.

I want the one I've settled on. I say so.

Flatly, with no trace of emotion, she says: "Okay. *But you can't do much better than this.*" She slips the paper into her pocket.

Now, what does she mean? *You can't do much better than this?* Does that mean the price is 5¢? Of course, I can't do *better* than that. On the other hand, most of the balloons are probably marked $1.00; consequently I can't do *much better* than $1.00.

She reaches for another balloon.

"Wait!" I grab her arm, perhaps a little too forcefully.

"I gotta think about this. I may go with pink."

"It's O.K." She pats my hand, and says in that sub-Saharan voice, "Take a second to decide."

I keep trying to figure out those balloons.

Meanwhile, Wanda sets about preparing my banana split.

Let me tell you something. Most waitresses make

orthodox banana splits. A few make Victorian banana splits. But Wanda's banana splits look like Disneyland. They have chambers of ice cream: vanilla, chocolate, strawberry. They have a chocolate roof with nut tiles. They have whipped cream minarets and cherry finials. They have a coconut lawn, and a moat full of thick pineapple syrup. They are built on solid banana.

She holds it up for my inspection. My mouth waters. My head circles, searching for a place to start in.

"I'm taking my lunch break," she says. "When I come back . . . I'll make you one of these."

She takes the slip of paper and a nickel from her pocket, drops it in the register. Then she takes a seat at the end of the counter and eats her banana split.

I watch the slow circles her head makes, looking for the first place to excavate. Watch her take in each spoonful, letting it liquefy in the warmth of her mouth, slip coolly down her throat. I watch her down to the last morsel, a stray half-pecan.

"Yeah! Back to work!!" I clap my hands and give her my broadest grin. "Hi, ho."

"Stop trying to humor me. I still got ten minutes on my break." Her voice has changed. There is fluidity to it now.

I get up and wander around. It really is a pretty nice 5¢ to $1.00 store. It has wooden plank floors and smells of orange circus peanuts.

When I return, a kid is sitting on my stool eagerly pointing to a green balloon.

"Hey! HEY!" I rush toward him. "I saw it first!"

Pop. Too late.

Wanda sets down her knife.

She opens the slip.

"Five cents."

Now I understand. *All* the green balloons are 5¢.

She makes him a breathtaking banana split. As she sets it down in front of him, his head begins circling, scanning the peaks and valleys. . . .

Wanda comes back.

"*I'd* like a green balloon," I demand.

"We're all out of bananas," she announces.

I guess I become a little hysterical. I plead with Wanda so desperately she finally sets about combing the luncheonette for a banana. She disappears into the backroom for a long long time, and I put my head down on the counter and dream of a ripe banana, its gown thrown aside, reclining on a glass dish. . . .

"I found this one. . . ." Wanda is shaking me awake. She dangles something between her thumb and index finger. Something black, overripe, between solid and liquid.

"That's not a banana anymore," I say.

Wanda is very understanding. She frees the last green balloon and hands it to me.

"There's another store out at the mall. Tell them Wanda Ledbetter said it's okay."

I walk back in the direction I'd come cradling the balloon. Past Edna's, the Family Steak House, the Health Hut. Tree branches lash out at the balloon. Car tires throw gravel at it.

It is four miles to the mall, inhabited mostly by fifteen-year-olds in Drivers License Limbo. Right before I reach the 5¢ to $1.00 one of them sticks a lit cigarette to the balloon. It explodes. The folded slip clicks to the floor. I reach down, pick it up, open it.

5¢.

Then I go into the 5¢ to $1.00.

I have the Tuna Special. Fat chunks of fresh tuna on crisp toast. I can taste the egg in the mayonnaise. I savor every snappy bit of celery. There are golden potato chips and a festive pickle.

"Good, huh?" asks the waitress, catching me using the magnetic part of the finger, the part that picks up crumbs.

"Good," I reply, satisfied.

The bill is 93¢. I tip her my last 7¢ and stroll out into the mall. Music plays. There is a hint of Climate-Control in the air. All across America it is Tuna Special Day.

SOME WOMEN I'VE KNOWN

People ask me if I ever get lonely on the road.

"It must be hard to meet women," they say.

If they only knew.

There was Elmira. And Odessa. And Enid.

I sat up all night talking civil rights with Selma. There was one from New Jersey—Elizabeth, I think her name was—who smoked too much. There was a fine southern beauty named Charlotte. And a midwestern rose: Abilene.

There was Ruth, Gretna, Hope, Ada, Cynthia, Beverly, Alexandria, Abby. There were four named Fayette and six named Florence.

There were exotic ones. Eufala, Opa Locka, Nanty Glo.

Legendary ones. Big Sandy and Little Nell, Upper Darby and Lower Marion. There was even one in the Tennessee backwoods they called Soddy Daisy.

Hey, I slept with Pocahontas and Princess Anne.

I slept with DeQueen.

Okay. Once in Oklahoma I spent the night with a Hooker.

•   •   •

I've slept on Davenports, Fossil Beds, Yellow Springs, Kennebunks, even a Tombstone. Once I woke up on May's Landing.

You never know just what kind of activity the night might entail. It may be a mild Kissimmee. It could be a French Lick, or a Lovelock. It could be a hell of a night.

I could wake up with Muscle Shoals or Horseshoe Bends, searching for the Medicine Lodge.

On the other hand, there might be a fine breakfast in bed. Salmon or Sandwich. Mayo or Hominy.

And then I'll be moving on. Thinking about those women. Their Great Neck. Their Sleepy Eye. Their Yellow Foot. Their Mouth of Wilson. Their Foggy Bottom.

Me, I don't try to figure them out.

They're Superior, Mystic, Normal, Bountiful, Picayune, Liberal, and sometimes Falmouth. I just try to appreciate them for what they are. Fine, fine American women, every one of 'em. Yessiree. Real Buttes.

FRED SUSS'S SHIP IN A CAN

EMPORIA, KANSAS.

"Let me get this right. You build ships in cans?"

"Yessir. That's right."

"Why?"

"It gets slow around here at night."

"No, why do you build them in cans?"

"I like cans."

"How long have you been doing this?"

"Well, let's see. It'd be close to thirty-five years, I believe. I built my first one right after they switched me over to security guard. Built it into a tomato juice can."

"Most people build ships in bottles."

"Yessir."

"Did you ever think about that? So that admirers could see them a little better?"

"Well, I always preferred cans. When I began, cans was tin. All my earliest models are in tin cans. I reckon they could be worth something. I've worked my way up from cans to drums. This . . . this one here . . . is the *Bonhomme Richard*. It's over a foot and a half long. Go ahead . . . hold it."

"Well, it . . . feels . . . like a ship's in there alright."

"Put it up to your ear. Shake it."

"Sounds pretty seaworthy. How long did it take you to build this?"

"Well, I throw the ships together in nothing flat. It's canning them that's the painstaking part. This drum took half a day. It's hand-welded. Those little, ribbed deals around it are called beads. I formed them myself."

"You seem proud of your craft."

"Yessir. I know my business. I've been at this canning company since 1936. Up until 1970 I was a bottom seamer. Then everything went aluminum, and they moved me to security. But I can still seal any kind of can you want. Tin, zinc, steel, electroplate . . . seal 'em near to human perfect. I dare you to find a nub on that can you're holding."

"It looks like very good work."

"Most people don't appreciate a good can. You ever been inside a Quonset Hut?"

"No."

"I like cans. Did you find any nubs?"

"No. It's a very smooth seal."

"Seamless. Yessir."

"It's been good talking with you. It's rare to find someone nowadays who takes pride in their work."

"Well, the best work is work you don't see at all."

THE HARDEST WORKING VOICE IN SHOW BUSINESS

LIMON, COLORADO.

Today I came across one of the all-time great voices of Show Business.

77

•   •   •

He is lying face up in some weeds. The fact that he has been severed seems somehow fitting. A lot of his work has been in horror films.

Someone must've traveled a ways before throwing him out.

No telling how long he has been lying there, rusting. Years maybe.

I pick him up.

If he hadn't been severed, he might've spoken to me.

His voice would be thin and cracked. Very monaural.

"Insensitive jerk. Just tossed me right out."

•   •   •

I decide to return him.

"Don't get me started," I almost heard him say. "I was the hardest working voice in Show Business.

"My day began at dusk, sometimes went all night. When that first car arrived, that was my cue. I opened up with some musical numbers . . . "Oh, Lonesome Me" by Jo Stafford, or maybe it was Eydie Gorme . . . "Ramblin' Rose" by Nat King Cole. Maybe a few instrumentals . . . Percy Faith or Nelson Riddle.

"And I would break up the songs with patter. You know . . . 'eight, eight, eight minutes to showtime folks!' Working the crowd up.

"I listened for the cars arriving, the crunch of tires on gravel, jockeying up to the poles. Kids would amble down to the screen, where there was a playground and free pony rides.

"And when it was officially dusk, when the last lightning bug went lights out, *that's* when the cartoon began. And the kids raced back and plopped themselves on the hoods of their parents' cars, or on a blanket on the gravel.

"Now let me tell you something. The drive-in movie was a bad idea from the start. But Americans did everything they could to make a good time of it. They put up with bars running down the middle of their windshields which split the movie in half. Planes flew overhead. People made shadowgraphs on the screen. I kept having to interrupt myself: Suddenly Richard Widmark would be mouthing, 'Attention, please, will the parents of Lisa—age four—*please* come to the snack bar?'

"Why did people keep coming? Because I gave 'em a show! Music. Previews. A cartoon. Two features. No one ever left complaining about not getting their money's worth!

"I did it all. I was the voice of Steve McQueen, Ben Hur, John Wayne, Billy Jack, Bambi, and Dumbo. I was the Unsinkable Molly Brown. I was Rodan, Reptilicus, the Fly . . . I was eight hundred Japanese extras screaming, 'Run for your lives, it's Godzilla. . . .'

"Sure, I know what kind of activity went on at Drive-Ins. On a few occasions, I inspired it. Remember Sandra Dee and Troy Donahue in *A Summer Place?*

$$\text{hmmm,}$$
hmmm, hmmm, hmmm, hmmm,
$$\text{hmmm, hmmm, hmmm,}$$
hmmm
$$\text{hmm}$$

"And, yes, I did a lot of horror flicks, which I wasn't crazy about. They're usually just plain dumb. The characters never pay attention to the titles. *Don't Answer the Door. Don't Look in the Basement.* If they paid attention to the titles, they wouldn't get hacked up, would they?

"Yeah, I did it all. . . .'' he would say in that underrated voice.

•   •   •

We arrive at the Sky-Vue. The marquee, with its mixed, mis-sized lettering, reads like a giant ransom note:

CLOSED
FLEA MARKET EVERY SUNDAY

The drive-in is an empty picketed landscape. The snack bar seems to be crouching, humiliated.

I walk over to the roped-off flea market. It isn't much—a few solemn vendors hawking merchandise of questionable repute. Digital grandfather clocks. Phony Rolexes. Louis LXIV Beanbag chairs.

One old fellow is sitting on the tailgate of his battered station wagon. Spread on a blanket at his feet are three items: a badminton racket, a ukulele, a can of Rust-Oleum.

"How much for the Rust-Oleum?"

"It's a set. I can't break it up."

I haggle. He agrees to let the Rust-Oleum go.

I clean up the speaker, choose a pole close to the screen, and set the speaker into a wire cradle. Then I search for the cable running just beneath the gravel. . . .

•　　　•　　　•

Dusk is settling as I head back toward the highway.

Then from behind, I can almost hear the strains of Nelson Riddle and his Orchestra. And then . . . unmistakably . . . Jo Stafford . . .

"*I've thought of everything from A to Z . . .*
Oh, lonesome meeeee. . . ."

Or maybe it is Eydie Gorme.

THWOP, THWOP

WISCONSIN DELLS, WISCONSIN

Nothing in Wisconsin Dells seems to be from Wisconsin Dells.

"Homemade!" cry all the souvenirs and tourist trinkets, but the genuine Wisconsin string cheese is from Canada, the labels on the "authentic" rubber-headed Chippewa tomahawks bear a curious rackjobber haiku:

FUN HATCHET TOY

There are more exclamation marks here than anywhere in America:

MYSTERY HOUSE!! SEE GRAVITY DEFIED!
WORLD-FAMOUS DANCING CHICKENS!!

(The chickens "dance" on an aluminum foil stage. There is a hotplate underneath.) The Ripley Museum exemplifies the town's attitude. "You can believe it or not. We don't care." Wisconsin Dells is lurid, like an aging showgirl, and it creaks with the sound of arthritic turnstiles.

In the middle of all this sits the bustling Affy-Tapple stand. Ruth Sosnick runs it with her six children. Family-operated. Family-owned.

"My oldest, Earl, was kind of mumble-mouthed," says Ruth, a widow. "He would say Affy-Tapple instead of Taffy Apple. It sort of caught on."

Each kid oversees a specific function. Rupert, 7, unloads the apples from crates. Deirdre, 12, "spots" them for bruises. Earl, 14, submerges each in a swirling bin of taffy, retrieves them, and moves them along the belt to Brenda, 9, who runs the dowel-punch. Terry, 10, rolls them in a gravel pit of crushed nuts. The once-scruffy winesaps are soon all creamy leather and nuggets.

But it is the sixth member of the operation, Randy, 11,

whose inspired contribution made Affy-Tapple Wisconsin Dell's most popular concession. At 6 p.m. all the unsold Affy Tapples are carried next door to an empty lot. The dowels are removed. Moments later, a dull, steady "thwop" fills the evening air.

"This is better than Fantasy Camp," beams Randy. Behind him, youngsters pick bits of apple out of their hair and anxiously await their turn at bat. Randy has his own explanation for the U-Swat-Em's success.

"Every ballplayer secretly dreams of hitting a ball so hard it explodes. Here it happens every time."

Thwop! Thwop!

"Swing for power. Not distance!" he instructs a toddler with an outsized bat.

Thwop.

The family-run business is an endangered commodity. Here in Wisconsin Dells, the steady sound of apples being pulverized seems a welcome reinstatement.

RIDICULOUS

LINTON, INDIANA.

I catch myself doing something I haven't done in years. Sneaking a look. You know the magazine I'm talking about.

The newsstand owner isn't watching.

It's kind of juvenile, sure. But I'd heard it was a great issue, and I just want to see for myself.

Funny, now that I'm old enough to afford the magazine, I never buy it. Sure, I'll look at a copy if it's lying around on a friend's table but. . . .

I inch closer, pick up a decoy magazine, a *Popular Mechanics.* Pretend to read an article on hydrofoils. Pretty hokey, I know.

There is a kid by the comics eyeing me. I feel a wash of embarrassment. He *knows* I'm gonna sneak a look. What the hell, he's probably sneaked a look himself.

Then I do it. Just shoot my arm out, grab the magazine, turn to *that* page and get my jollies.

Naturally, others have already beat me to it. The page is all creased.

Which takes away a little of the excitement, the private reward of discovery.

Still, it makes me laugh. Out loud. It is a very good *MAD* Magazine Ridiculous Fold-In.

"Hope you don't mind, it's a little manhandled," says Morland, the newsstand owner. Feeling a tincture of guilt, I have decided to pay for the magazine.

"It's OK. How much do I owe you?"

"One thirty-five," he says, and then inexplicably shouts, "CHEAP!!" loudly enough to cause several heads to turn.

•   •   •

•   •   •

The more I think about the Ridiculous Fold-In, the more it merits reexamination. It seems to me a brilliant literary device. I cross the street to the Linton Public Library.

© 1986 by E. C. Publications, Inc.

"Do you have an *Encyclopedia of English Terms & Usages*?" I ask the librarian, who is peeling Elmer's from her fingers.

She gives an exaggerated sigh, disappears, and returns pushing the book on a dessert tray.

I look up "Ridiculous Fold-In" in *The Encyclopedia of English Terms & Usages*.

It's right there between Rhyme Scheme and Rising Action.

". . . there seems to be some divisiveness as to the origin of the Ridiculous Fold-In. Mumford (*Technics and Civilization*, 1934) attributes it to the estimable Alfred E. Neuman. However, the *Harvard Guide to Contemporary American Writing* (1940) cites a well-known-at-the-time school of dissidents calling themselves The Usual Gang of Idiots. . . ."

No matter. What is important is its validity.

I remember once taking an entire course on *Ulysses*. "What does it mean?" was the course's objective and at semester's end no one could yet say for sure.

"Where can I find *Ulysses*?" I ask the librarian.

"U.S. History: Civil War," she replies, rolling her eyes. I let it go.

I find it eventually.

A paperback version. Published by someone called Medusa Press.

Out of curiosity I look at the lending card to see who in this town has read *Ulysses*.

Someone named Dr. Clarence Runion has read *Ulysses*. Twice.

A James Pennegar has read *Ulysses*.

There is only one other name. Kevin. Thickly penciled. Small k. Backward n.

I turn to the last page of the book, the page where, with uncharacteristic jocularity, Joyce has penned this cryptic dénouement:

> **A**   **B**
> **Whatever your reading preference, we hope that
> Medusa Books will be your choice. We ship
> Worldwide. Allow 6–8 weeks for delivery.**

I glance around. The librarian isn't looking.

I "fold B to where it meets A." And I understand then what Joyce is trying to say when he speaks of the "incertitude of the void. . . ."

I'm not the first. Kevin has beaten me to it.

"ZING"

CHILLICOTHE, OHIO.

I stand in the spot where Zing was. Earlier today they took Zing away.

For thirty years he stood in the corner of the basement Vend-o-Mat of the Ohio Insurance Building, dispensing refreshments to thirsty stenographers and office workers. He worked hard to make sure the drinks were always cold. He always offered a varied selection. In later years he clanked and creaked a lot, and his teeth had worn down to the point where you sort of had to help him gum the drinks open. But he still served faithfully.

And for only 10¢.

Zing was the last 10¢ Coke machine in America.

Folks called him Zing because that's what was printed on his sides: "Zing! What a feeling!" That was once one of Coca-Cola's catchphrases.

Used to be soft drinks had a small friendly attitude toward life. Pepsi emphasized politeness ("Say Pepsi, Please"), and Coke promised little moments of incandescence (Zing!). Then they got a little bolder. Politeness turned into aggression.

Soon Pepsi claimed an entire generation, and Coke decided it would try to teach the entire world to sing.

Zing wasn't interested in teaching folks to sing. He simply

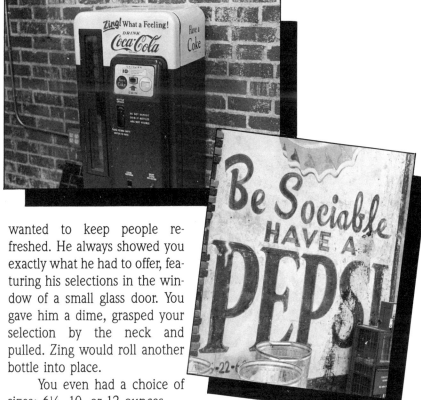

wanted to keep people refreshed. He always showed you exactly what he had to offer, featuring his selections in the window of a small glass door. You gave him a dime, grasped your selection by the neck and pulled. Zing would roll another bottle into place.

You even had a choice of sizes: 6½, 10, or 12 ounces.

Zing's only request was that you returned the empties. For your convenience, there was a small wooden crate nearby.

The office building employees kept Zing's existence a secret. Long after Cokes had risen to 50¢, Zing stayed hidden in the Vend-o-Mat, serving them up for a mere dime.

A sympathetic distributor kept him supplied, absorbing the loss out of his own pocket.

But then last week something happened. Old Zing kept someone's dime.

He probably didn't mean to. He was just getting old.

But whoever lost his dime worked him over pretty good.

They stuck a finger in his coin-return slot and tried to gag him. They kicked him.

Then they did the worst thing you can do to a drink machine. They humiliated him in public.

They taped a sign to him:

This Machine Owes Me 10 Cents!!

As if they expected Zing to personally pay them back.

It happened again the next day. Zing accidentally kept another dime. Someone else pasted a note on him.

And again and again. By the end of the week, Zing was covered with payment notes. He was in serious, serious debt.

People had quickly forgotten all those bargain 10¢ drinks.

•   •   •

Today, the sympathetic distributor came and took him away. Probably for his own safety. Someone had kicked a big dent into his side.

•   •   •

I stand in the Vend-o-Mat and stare at the stained square of flooring where Zing had been for thirty years. I really wish I had gotten there earlier to enjoy one of his 10¢ Cokes.

I always thought Coke tasted better from a bottle.

I would have chosen the 6½-ounce size. I would have downed it in one or two long gulps, then turned it over and examined the bottom. And whatever city was written there, that's where I would have headed next.

HOME

SPORTS ITEM:
(CINCINNATI, OHIO, RIVERFRONT STADIUM)

In a daring display of basepath wizardry, Richard Hall stole home from home today.

It happened in the fourth inning at Riverfront Stadium while the rest of the team was in Pittsburgh playing the Pirates. Hall bolted for first, rounded the basepath, and with a spectacular head-first dive, baptized himself in the dust of home plate.

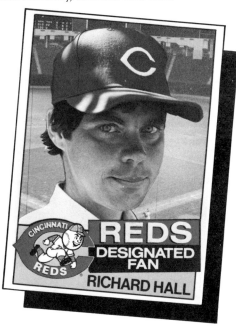

"It was a dream come true," he remarked afterward, pausing to relish the feverish roar emanating from within his cupped hands.

Hall, who has a lifetime contract with the Reds as a Designated Fan, entered the stadium through an open "Person-

93

nel Only" door when no one was looking.

"I didn't think I'd get as far as I did," he said. "I kept thinking someone was going to stop me."

Miraculously, Hall found himself standing at home plate with no one around.

What was it like? he was asked.

"Like standing at the bottom of a Chinese checker board.

"I looked up and saw in each tiny colored square my own smallness. (This statement is characteristic of Hall's modesty. He has handled a variety of positions ably: General Admission, Loge, and Box.)

"Every step around the path kicked up the dust of memories. My uncle used to take me to the Reds games when they played at Crosley field. There was a terrace at the wall, a real guerrilla advantage. There was ivy, and real grass, and those stark white delineations—'lime' they called it and you always tried to picture that strange process of extraction. There was the smell of warm beer; brands that never got out of Cincinnati. Exotic and Germanic and allegiant. Wiedemann, Hudepohl, Oertels '92, Burger. . . .

"I remember singing 'Take Me Out to the Ballgame . . .' that paean to Gluttony ('buy me some peanuts and crackerjacks . . .') Apathy ('I don't care if I never get back . . .') Nihilism ('One . . . Two . . . Three strikes you're OUT!').

"Mostly, I remembered the roar of the crowd. It was a surging, explosive squall that physically lifted you from your seat.

"I learned to re-create that sound, a curious respiratory trick.

I used it when I circled the little league fields after the games, when the crowds were dwindling and dusk advanced.

"I used it when perfecting my famous Roof Diving catches." (Richard Hall invented the pastime of throwing a ball onto a roof, circling the house and diving for it as it came down the other side.)

"I used it during the Firefly Practice" (the intense fifteen minutes at twilight when lightning bugs tried to avoid Richard's savage Whiffle Bat).

"I played that sound all through my life, expanded it to functions beyond baseball. In Study, in Sex, in life's clutch plays, I often let that roar fill my head, a private standing ovation.

"And now, I was hearing it again as I rounded third and barreled for home.

"A groundskeeper had spotted me by now.

"He was yelling at me, but, of course, I couldn't hear him. Not with that roar.

"It was close.

"I had to dive. To close my eyes and hurl myself forward, and with the very edge of my fingertips, find that cool rubbery pentagon, that ultimate and finite Point on the Earth, and pull it towards me.

"Home.

"The crowd went wild."

·   ·   ·

In an achievement that surpasses his once catching two foul balls at Riverfront Stadium, Richard Hall stole home from home today.

Afterward, security personnel lifted him and carried him out of the stadium.

GLENN

PERU, VERMONT.

"Climb on."

"Serious?"

"Sure. I could use the heft. Watch your trousers."

We head straight uphill. I watch a bandoleer of veins form on the back of his neck.

"Try to pedal in sync!" he calls. His voice sounds like a wheezy western sidekick. "Else you're fighting me the whole way."

The hill tops out beside a pasture of bluebells. Mottled cows eye us, chew listlessly. The terrain dictates the conversation.

"Can I ask you a question?" I say, when we start the steep descent.

"You just did."

"Did you lose someone along the way?"

"Now, how did I know you were gonna ask me that? Yeah, my wife. We signed up for one of those fourteen-day bed and breakfast tours."

I had seen the ad. A tiny frame in the back of the *New York Times Magazine*.

"After the first day, I had to leave her behind. . . . Newfane, I think it was."

"Why?"

"These inns are thirty, forty miles apart. I did some nood-ling with the calculator. Distance times calories times money times fourteen. No question about it, we would have starved to death. The only way to come out ahead is to get in three, four breakfasts a day."

We reach the bottom of the hill and dismount.

"What about sleep?"

"I nap for a few hours, move on," he says. "By and large, the beds are too lumpy anyway." From his seat pocket he ex-tracts a moist guide pamphlet, peels open a page. The flush on his face is subsiding like thermometer mercury.

"No. 12. *The Okemo Inn*," he reads, and peers down the road, as if squinting hard enough will bring it closer:

> "'A painstakingly restored Victorian home that features *eight* roaring fireplaces.'"

In Glenn's wire bike basket there are T-shirts, underwear, socks, a can of Dial, a tube of Colgate, a toothbrush, and a giant bran muffin. He pulls it out, picks some lint from it.

"Last of 'em," he says, offering me half.

We dine among the bluebells.

A milktruck—the old-fashioned kind with haunches, two square eyes, a high, rounded forehead, a snaggletoothed bumper—rattles by, honks its horn, and disappears beneath a red covered bridge. Everything in Vermont you've seen before on jigsaw puzzles.

He continues reading from the guide pamphlet:

"'Breakfasts at the Okemo are sumptuous and delightful! Try Barbara's Homemade & Sinful pastries. Afterward you can retire to the quiet, cozy parlor where Tom will happily regale you with a story or two of the Okemo's vivid past.'"

"How can the parlor be quiet with eight roaring fireplaces?" Glenn says.

"You from New York City?" I ask.

"Shows that bad, hunh?"

"No. Strictly a guess."

He lifts up a shirtsleeve, taps at his forearm, making pink blotches.

"I know. I got a tan like Liquid Paper. What can I do? I work in the financial district. It's all canyons."

"What do you do?"

"Satellites." He says this as if the word were all-inclusive and whips out a business card:

GLENN PETRIE   PETRIE SATELLITE SERVICES
14 WILLIAMS ST. N.Y.C.

The card shows a satellite dish and little cartoon wavelengths. It is made of thin, indestructible plastic.

"How's business?"

"Business is business. You gotta wake up every morning and shout, 'Carpe Diem!' "

He pronounces it as if it were a subphylum.

"That means 'seize the day.' You gotta scratch and bleed, scratch and bleed. But up here, my God . . ." He inhales lustily. "I dunno. Maybe I won't go back."

And he lifts his head and shouts in the direction of New York City two hundred miles away:

"No, no, you *can't* fire me. I quit!!

"C'mon," he says, climbing back on the bike.

We pedal off again, passing under the covered bridge. In the picketed light he calls out:

"You'd think after two hundred years they'd know how to make a weatherproof bridge."

Like all Bed & Breakfast owners, you cannot think of Ted & Barbara without the ampersand. The house seems to have joined them at the hip.

Ted greets us. He looks like the Rifleman, and when you look closely you see wrinkles, like shutters, gathered at his eyes.

"Welcome to the Okemo!" he says. There is sweat on his lip. Maintaining eight fireplaces is like spinning plates.

Barbara is not evident. I figure she is in the kitchen somewhere conjuring sinful pastries.

"This the place with the 'Big & Thirsty towels'?" asks Glenn, remembering something he read in the pamphlet.

"No, that's the Ransome House. Ours are kind of soft and nubby." He reaches for Glenn's loose belongings.

"I'll show you . . . fellas . . . um, gentlemen . . . to the room."

Glenn taps his watch.

"Tell you what, Ted. We're kinda pressed. If it's all the same to you, we'll just chow down and be on our way."

.   .   .

3:45 p.m. Breakfast. Ted & Barbara sit at the table with us, arms crossed tightly, watching Glenn commandeer his fourth breakfast of the day.

The food is double-adjective delicious.

"I'll have another light & fluffy omelette," he says, extending his plate. His free hand probes a napkin-lined basket.

"Where'd those sinful & homemade pastries get to?"

"You ate them all."

Glenn settles for one more buttery & mouthwatering flapjack.

"Hey, Ted . . ." he says between forkfuls, "the inn guide mentions some 'painstaking restoration.' Sounds like there might've been some juicy accidents."

Ted is tight-lipped, worried. Tempering the griddle at 3:45 to make Glenn's flapjacks will mean a rubbery dinner for the other guests.

Barbara excuses herself to pack us some pastries for the road.

"You've got a smart operation here, Ted," Glenn says, chiseling the last speck of egg from his plate.

"Yeah," Ted replies, and pours himself another cup of thick & bracing coffee. "Everyday's a rent party."

•   •   •

Halfway between Okemo and Sandwort, on Route 7, there is a stand of maples, fronted by a small log cabin. The cabin was built by Josh and Stuart Lingerfelt six years ago. From a distance, it appears to be constructed of tootsie rolls. It is the home of the Circadia Corporation.

Glenn bounds off the porch, snapping a certificate between his hands, testing its resiliency.

"Look at this . . ." he beams, flagging the paper at me, "my own little piece of Vermont."

The certificate entitles Glenn to one lifetime maple syrup timeshare.

For two weeks out of the year all the syrup tapped from a particular tree will be shipped to Glenn in New York.

"What did you pay for this?" I ask.

"Nothing. I traded out. One satellite dish . . . one lifetime share of syrup."

We pedal toward Sandwort. Eventually a steeple appears.

There are more steeples in Vermont than anywhere in America. They are always the first thing to draw the eye, white, severely angled, assuring.

In Vermont there are no skyscrapers. The steeple is always the tallest structure.

At each town, Glenn tries to convince the rector his steeple is the perfect place to install a satellite receiving dish.

· · ·

The police catch up with Glenn on the other side of Sand-wort.

There is no wife, no satellite distributorship. He has paid for the bed & breakfast tour with a bogus check. They put him in a kind of paddywagon shaped not unlike those covered bridges we kept passing under.

"No . . . no . . . you don't understand . . ." he says as they're handcuffing him, "you *can't* arrest me. I'm turning my-self in."

They strap the bike to the top of the van, and drive off.

"Carpe Diem," I call after him. Crook or no crook, you have to admire anyone who can cram two weeks into three days.

· · ·

Later I check out Glenn's business card. The address be-longs to a Tae Kwan Do parlor in lower Manhattan. Now, once a year, its owner curiously receives several quarts of genuine Ver-mont maple syrup.

THE UGLIEST TOWN IN AMERICA

Marilyn Monroe sat in my lap.
It happened in Atlantic City, New Jersey.

·   ·   ·

The first time I see her she is climbing behind the wheel of a Vega in the parking lot of Two Guys Department Store. She slides a plastic bag of discount cosmetics onto the seat beside her and wheels by, just as I'm stepping out of the Trailways.

I recognize the pout. The beauty mark. The explosion of blondeness.

She doesn't see me at all.

The Trailways disgorges its passengers. They reel momentarily in the brilliance of coastal light, clutch their plastic slot cups to their chests. They look like a convention of Slurpee drinkers.

None of them had seen her.

Some town, Atlantic City.

"I just saw Marilyn Monroe," I say to the driver. It's OK to talk to him now, the vehicle is not in motion.

He lets the bus answer for him, a weary hydraulic sigh.

Someone herds us toward another bus. This one has a casino's name on it. In Atlantic City, you don't necessarily arrive at a bustling terminal. More than likely, it's a parking lot on the outskirts. A motel, a bowling alley, a Two Guys. Then, as if in a hostage drama, you're transferred to another bus, kept perpetually addled.

The ride to the casino is punctuated with quick annoyed exchanges:

"Lean back. I can't see out."

"There's nothing to see. It looks like Dresden."

"Give me the Vicks."

"Why? What is it?"

"Give me the Vicks."

"You want me to open the window?"

"Give me the Vicks."

"My left hand is itching. That's a good sign."

"Look. Vic Damone at the Sands. Did I ever tell you I met Vic Damone? When I was an MP?"

"That was Victor Mature."

A beer bottle shuttles up and down the aisle, jangling against the metal seat supports. No one bothers to pick it up.

From the bus window, I look for Marilyn. She is nowhere to be found. In fact, there are no good-looking people anywhere in Atlantic City. Figures, sadly postured, skirt the broken glass and upheaved sidewalks, their eyes buried cavelike in parka hoods. A stray German shepherd turns warily at the approach of a combat-booted bantamweight who throws punches at an invisible opponent. The dog scurries toward an empty lot; its feet move twice as fast as its torso. There are hollow buildings bandaged with plywood. There is a rescue mission with a sign in the parking lot:

But there is no Marilyn Monroe.

There are no good-looking people in the casinos. Faces are sullen, bulbous, big-pored, women apply makeup with a leaden hand, men comb their hair in odd contours that resemble Andean plowing techniques. Tans are by QT, even though the beach is right outside the door.

There are no good-looking people here.

What turns the head is sudden movement. The stutter step of quick fortune, a craps winner leaping Varsity Girl style—percolated joy in his throat.

Otherwise there is no wasted motion. People speak with their hands, a wave for yes, a tap for no. And, always there is the din, the dissonance, the jangling of change thrown down. There are no windows. No clocks.

No good-looking people.

It's quite a phenomenon.

This is why, once a year, they cart in fifty-one of the most beautiful women in America and parade them around—to remind everyone in Atlantic City there are still some good-looking people out there.

•   •   •

I finally find her.

Marilyn Monroe.

She is in the Legends In Concert revue at one of the casinos. Along with Elvis, the Beatles, Buddy Holly, Al Jolson, Judy Garland.

It isn't as bad a show as it sounds. George Harrison is a little chunky, kind of like Raymond Burr, and Buddy Holly looks less like Buddy Holly and more like the guy who used to play Dennis the Menace's dad. But there is a lot of energy.

And Marilyn steals the show.

She is sultry and diaphanous; the heavy-lidded stare, the splayed fingers, shoulders thrown back, that eerie walking-under-water effect are all uncannily perfect. For a brief moment I suspect fraud. I've heard the best Marilyn impersonators are men.

But during the "My Heart Belongs to Daddy" number,

when she comes off the stage and right by my table—so close I can feel the satin breeze—I know she is all woman. She smells faintly of coconut.

There is an old guy, somebody's granddad, at the next table. She floats him onstage to a wooden chair, pushes him down, pours herself onto his lap. He can only sit there with his false teeth bared in a sheepish grin, his ears appearing to grow larger.

Men whistle, women gasp, the old guy's wife takes Instamatic photos.

I'd have given anything to be in his place.

· · ·

I stay for the late show, jockey for the old man's table, thinking maybe Marilyn always chooses that spot.

She chooses another old guy. He is wearing a Mets cap and she leads him up on stage by its bill. The other old guys at his table get a big kick out of it. There will be some talk back home.

She leads him by my table. He is smoking a stubby White Owl. It should smell putrid. But it doesn't. It smells like coconuts.

· · ·

Reboarding the casino bus, in the dark, the people's movements are slow, weary, defeated. Men walk ahead of their wives, sullenly.

"You shoulda told me. The moment your hand stopped itching, you shoulda said something."

On the floor of the bus there is a discarded piece of paper with hundreds of numbered configurations, meticulously columned. Somebody kicks the same beer bottle and it glances off my heel.

The bus starts to pull away, then jerks to a stop. Doors hiss, a silhouetted figure moves through the aisle, using her overnight case for balance. As she nears I can smell coconuts.

Maybe she was tired of being the only good-looking person in Atlantic City. Maybe, like me, she couldn't wait to get back to a small town, a normal place. Maybe she got a better part.

All I know is just as she passed me, the bus gave a rude, violent lurch. . . .

•   •   •

Marilyn Monroe sat in my lap.
It happened in Atlantic City, New Jersey.

LUCY

NEW YORK CITY.

The Statue of Liberty.

It seems a fitting place to end my journey.

I know it sounds sappy, but I really want to see her up close: to see her massiveness, the true weight of her promise; to see that torch, an eternal beacon for travelers everywhere. "Give me your tired, your poor, your huddled masses. . . ." she proclaims.

Most newcomers to America still arrive in New York, though nowadays it's usually by plane.

The Poor get off first, followed by the Tired, then the Huddled Masses, who must be kept huddled, a difficult organizational feat. Then some maintenance-type people go on and collect all the Wretched Refuse.

The arrivees are shuttled to Immigration & Naturalization where they are issued a green card and a surly stare from an Immigration official who clearly is fed up with Tired, Poor, Huddled Masses and wouldn't mind seeing a few Rich, Preppy types show up.

I never make it to the Statue. There are no back roads into New York City and the Bridge and Toll people won't let me cross on foot.

In Margate City, New Jersey, I find my own beacon of welcome.

Lucy is not as massive as Lady Liberty, nor does she vaunt the anthemic posture. She appears to be made of some kind of roofing material, and there are windows in her sides that hint she may have once been part of a bad theme restaurant.

Yet to me, freshly, happily displaced, she represents a never-forgetting promise of America, the freedom to build your dreams, no matter how big and goofy those dreams are.

About a hundred yards from Lucy is a miniature golf concession.

Immediately after viewing Lucy, I report to the golf hut. There I am issued a putter, a gaily colored ball and (because it is Tuesday night) a two for one pass. All for sixty cents.

I play a round, something I haven't done in years. And in those eighteen holes, I discover a microcosm of America itself; a place of gentle green and clear gurgling waters, of good light and unexpected curves. A place of imagination. Of moving wind-mills, prehistoric creatures whose eyes actually light up; a place where everything is Smaller than Life and Bigger than Life at the same time.

At each hole I reach into the cup and retrieve my ball. Except the last.

Here the ball drops over the lip and disappears forever.

I've always wondered where all those balls go.

SPECIAL THANKS TO...

Jackson Browne; John F. Stolle and Bear Automotive Service Equipment Company; *MAD* magazine and its publisher, Bill Gaines; the Cincinnati Reds and their owner Marge Schott and Schottzie; Cincinnati Riverfront Stadium; the Coca-Cola Company and Philip F. Mooney; Sharon DeVall (Monroe) "Legends In Concert," pictured on page 106; California Snack Foods; Rodriguez Candy Apples; the Joseph M. Herman Shoe Company, Inc.; *The Herald*, Snohomish County, Washington; Anthony Salcido and the Glendale Batting Cage; Ben Bennett; Vic Lowrey; Dave Pearlberg; Tom Voelpel; Bob and Linnea Wentworth; Maggie Irwin; Steven and Margie Hess; Ted Steinberg; Earl and Yolanda Strode; Kirk Findley; Mark Thompson; Herbert N. Alexander; Lee H. Stanley; Sterling Christensen; Rick and Barbara Spilberg; Jaime, Jody, John and Barbara Olsen; Elaine and Ryan Brueckner; Melinda, Lindy and Marvin Sobel; May Sonnenberg; Henry Goldstrom; David P. Becker; Tom Warwick; Carl Rasmussen; Dr. James Fox; Barbara Allred; Pastor Randy Horton; Chuck McCue.

Thanks to Bob Pook for cover photo and art direction.

And Especially to . . .

Bonnie Burns

Katherine Meyer